Hello?

Poems on Fear

Leanna Amos

First published in Great Britain in 2019 by Sleepy Lion
Publishing

Text Copyright © Leanna Amos, 2019
Interior Illustrations Copyright © Leanna Amos 2019

Cover Illustration Copyright © Leanna Amos 2019

ISBN: 978-1-9160012-9-9

SLEEPY LION
PUBLISHING

www.sleepylionpublishing.com

Also by Leanna Amos:

Poems on Life Series:

Hello? Poems on Fear

Poems on Beauty
 (Coming soon)

Poems on Art
 (Coming soon)

Prelude

Every poem is a moment, a glimpse into an experience. The writing of each poem has been a unique occurrence, spanning over several years, usually a voice that felt the need to be expressed or as an answer to a question I'd asked the world when I felt most alone. Poetry has been my guide, a leading hand and a reason to wonder, and this is what I wish it brings to you.

Throughout this book you will notice a curious little character joining you alongside my poetry. His name is Beeboo and, put simply, he is a metamorphic podgy white lump. He is also very curious and full of emotion; he dwells in feeling and wonders a lot. At the back of the book you'll find his story.

"We are more often
frightened than hurt;
and we suffer more
from imagination
than from reality."

- Seneca

Monster

How does one

Escape their own fear?

The source of this danger

Feels incredibly near.

Please leave me alone,

I beg on my knees.

Can't you see me,

Down here,

Asking you please?

I can't take this feeling,

This fear is so strong.

I can't tell if you'll hurt me,

I don't know if I'm wrong.

It's tempting to look you

Right eye to eye,

But then maybe I'd face the truth,

The truth that this fear

Is an illusory lie.

Those who decided

I am grateful,
For every human adversity,
Conquered.

For every brave soul
Which surpasses
Their fears.

To those who try,
Even when they think
They cannot.

I live in the footsteps
Of those who took risks,
And those who decided to believe.

Given up

You may have thought

You'd given up,

But that's never true,

Unless you accept it.

You can pick yourself up,

Again, and again.

Every time you fall,

Laugh,

Then life will realise

You're just playing the game.

Start here

Start here,

Start by sitting up.

The day is never over

The day is never over,
You can always start again.
Stop listening to those thoughts
My dear.

Begin before
The voice comes in
To tell you not to
Embrace him.

You know what's right,
You know what to do,
Take this time right now
To take a step into life
And start again.

I'm terrified

My face burned,
Bright red,
It glowed.

The terror,
Insurmountable,
I climbed.

It's brave,
To be scared,
And carry on.

Tears

I'm not afraid to cry,

Not anymore.

Mystery

Life is a mystery,

Living is playing,

Problems are games.

There is no reason

To shy away;

So, delve in

And play.

Achievements

Your life is not:

- A,
- List,
- Of,
- Achievements.

Never Promised

Sometimes I'm scared,

To say goodnight,

To everything,

I see.

To leave my room behind,

For a universe,

Of dreams.

To leave the physical world,

For a land that's purely fictional.

To a place that's never promised.

Swim in these brave seas

I want emotional waves,

To crash and retreat.

To dive into an ocean.

To dive so deep.

I want a silence to surround.

FOLLOWED BY CROWDS IN YOUR
EARS.

I want to give you,

The permission,

To get rid,

Of your fears.

Look after yourself

You can't pour

From an empty cup;

Look after yourself.

Dreamer

It really doesn't matter,
How late you start.
If you've got a dream,
Then you have till you die.

One small step,
In the way you've always pictured.

You can go as far,
As anyone has dreamed of.

You're the one to achieve
The not quite possible.
You must have always known
It's better dreaming bigger.

Ghosts

Our fears are just ghosts,

That tell intricate lies.

Their stories convince us,

To hide from our lives.

Why am I scared?

It's scary,

Because the darkness,

It draws you in.

It's scary,

Because it is unknown,

Unfamiliar.

It's scary,

Because life has never

Granted us,

With an answer.

Misery

The misery is not

In the fear,

In the anxiety,

In the challenge,

In the problem.

The misery

Is in never having tried to overcome them,

And constantly being left with

What you know,

What you can do,

And who you already are.

Cathartic Monsters

I'll show you,
Because I'm scared.
You won't know this haunts me,
Yet it grasps my freedom,
It leaves me empty.

This catharsis,
It's a struggle.
Every moment's
Inner trouble.

A fear that leaves you dreaming,
Or stripped totally bare.
I have a choice,
To keep on leaving,
Or enter Evil's lair.

Constantly running

I'd spent a lot of time wanting to do
Everything.
Constantly in a hurry
To beat the next person.

Constantly running
Towards perceived perfection,
Whilst forgetting that my love truly lay
In a space which couldn't be rushed,
Which couldn't be hurried.

Time could never run out for those things.
You will never be late,
For what's real.

Alive

Feeling this much might hurt,

but my god do I feel alive.

Don't Lose Yourself

Portray yourself

As you will,

Although remember

Not to lose yourself,

In this pretty farce.

For underneath,

There are stories.

There are lies you cannot hide.

Reality Check

My bedroom
Was a reality check.
A familiar setting,
Returning every night,
Before the lights go out.

A glimpse into each corner
When I'm most alone,
Can leave me lost
In a place I've always known.

Consoling myself
With inner speeches
Of unchecked facts.
It can be so hard to bear.

Wake up

To wake up,

To my other life;

The one not in my dreams,

Where things make less sense,

The air is more dense,

Where I'm back trying to please.

A Perfect Prison

My perfectionism,
Was a prison.
It kept me away,
Years at a time.

I'd hear the keys rattle,
Nearby.
I'd feel hopeful, I'd dream,
Yet still, I could see.

There was comfort,
Staying still.
In pain.

An addiction, it became.

So hard

Sometimes...

    It's just,

        so Hard.

    But...

  I know,

I'll be, just,

    Fine.

Chisel away

I am on a path,

To chisel away,

Every fear.

To shape,

Every challenge.

To carve,

Every uncertainty.

Until,

Myself,

Is revealed.

Blame the Fire

Did I leave the candle burning?

Will I burn this house down?

Who'd be to blame,

If this went up in flames?

You don't have to run

So, stop avoiding
What seems hard.

You don't have to run
From what makes you feel
Alive.

No-one's around

Become more like you are,

When no one's around.

Thank you

You looked so confused,

So unknowing,

When you saw me being true.

I had let go of everything,

In front of you.

This was the closest to me you'd ever see.

So, remember to cherish the memory,

As you look back,

Because when I come to think of it,

I thank you for being there

And showing me who I was meant to be.

Courage

Lead me where

I feel least comfortable,

These are the places where

I become most humble.

Hedonism

I've found pleasure outside of hedonism;
I've found pleasure through pain
And fear.

Through all the things
They tell you never to meet,

That's where I found myself.

Honest

I've decided

To face the consequences,

Of being

Honest.

Laugh

If you're feeling overwhelmed,
Laugh at yourself.

Laugh at the way
Life isn't serious.
Laugh at the way
Things seem to happen.

Laugh at the reality
That you're here
Experiencing.

You got it

You got what
You told them.
You got what
You thought,
You believed.

So,
Of course,
That's what
You received.

Anyone

You're not fooling

Anyone.

Different Faces

We all wear different faces,

To the person inside,

Depending on who we're facing

On the outside.

Death

I drove myself crazy,

Thinking of not existing.

Something unescapable,

Yet subtly charming.

The world's greatest of mysteries,

And seriously grand.

A one-way street

Of the untouched snow,

A pure, white land.

I'll be okay

A tangle in my mind,

Thoughts caught in time.

Hate circulating,

Within me,

Within humankind.

I can't seem to escape,

This locked room,

Within me.

Wherever I go,

I'm blind,

I can't see.

I'm lost,

And I'm busy.

I feel pressure,

Within me.

It feels like I'm drowning,

In imaginary seas.

A crowd, in my head.

It felt loud,

As I've said.

Yet it all got so much,

I took a step back,

And a long,

Deep,

Breath.

It's okay,

I said to myself today.

I have nowhere to go.

These thoughts are just passing,

So,

Everything's fine,

Whatever the matter.

I'm loved,

And I'm here.

I've a purpose,

To exist,

And that's easy to do.

Any more is great,

But above that,

One thing,

And that thing is,

Be you.

Swings are for Adults

Do you dare,

To enter a playground?

A place of immediate joy.

Or would you rather,

Stay sulking?

Thinking,

I've lived too long,

Now this I can't.

Whose stopping you?

I ask.

Why this fear?

For there's places of bliss,
Unbelievably near.

Swings are for adults,
Not just garden furniture.
An experience, a feeling,
A motion-like curvature.

I can sense you are busy.
With what?
May I ask?

Is there more importance,

In such meaningless tasks?

Your soul's not on fire.
You're buried in thought.
All those desires,
You've simply got caught.

If you'll open your eyes,
Take a good look around.
Stop thinking, start feeling,
Take your feet off the ground.

Maybe you'll realise,
Swings are for adults.

Drag it through the mud

Take that fear

And drag it through the mud

Backwards,

If that's what it takes.

Time

I cannot see time;

Yet, time watches me.

Childhood

Conditioned.

Disciplined.

'Be yourself',

But obey.

Go on, be individual,

Imitate me,

Be like me,

But different, and better.

Volume

I'm amazed

How much I turn the volume down

When I'm not alone.

Excuses

You don't need to make excuses

In case someone's been watching.

Regardless

The energy you give off,
Will mean more than anything.

Regardless of how long it took
To style your hair,
Whether your walk is perfect,
Or those heels hold you high;

You'll always be the person,
You show up as.
You'll be
How you treat yourself,
And others.

If you compromise

Yourself,

It'll show through everything

You've built.

It'll wear on your face

So deep in your eyes.

Those Voices That You Hear

Your mind is playing

Tricks on you,

My dear.

Those voices that you hear,

Are nowhere near.

Whilst in the silence,

You tried to listen.

Yet the only noises

You could comprehend,

Where the distant sounds,

The voices of your friends.

It hurts

It's easy to stay stuck in misery,

It hurts,

But in there

I get comfortable.

Sheer Danger

Was this a fear,

I'd never considered?

Was it so blatant?

Was all I had,

Today?

Why was I running?

Speed at a hundred,

Miles.

Why was I hoping?

Prayers masking,

Lies.

I never expected,

To need bravery, for this.

Which I guess is why,

It never was, on my list.

Grasping onto anything,

Where I might feel something new.

Forgetting to turn around,

To realise,

I have something real.

Why

I knew I was right

But why

Was I so hard to believe?

Asking, Asking, Asking

It was one of those days,

When no matter how many men,

You came to pass and ask,

There was an unsatisfactory answer,

In the depth of their lips.

You listened for hours,

To anyone who could offer an opinion.

Whilst also keeping quiet,

As those you loved,

Stayed in the shadows of your thoughts.

You would surround yourself,

With bitter chat;

With sensory pleasures,

All to numb you,

As you wait.

You finally sat,

All alone.

As you had already been, amongst friends.

The noise had been so loud,

That now, it fell, suddenly.

You came to realise,

These questions,

As those which cannot be asked,

As those which are only felt,

Deeply within oneself.

It was on that same day,

You finally stopped asking.

Crashing Down

And my whole world

Came crashing down,

But with beauty

And grace.

It dissolved

Right in front of me,

All that I knew

As this separate body.

Where I realised

I began to realise,
The things I would fight most,
Were where I needed to let go.

Where I held most expectation,
Was where I needed
To be grateful
For where I am.

Where the places my mind
Would interrupt
And ruin,
Were where I could most
Bring love and compassion.

Where the people

I would judge

And criticize,

Were where I realised that I was only

Away from myself.

Hurt

I'm not scared of getting hurt,
Not now.

No one to blame

You begin to realise,

This really is what you make it.

There's no one here to blame,

Whether you're stuck where you are

Or going insane,

You've always had the power.

Take the paths that ignite you,

Don't waste time in fear.

Fear is a liar,

You know it too well,

It'll twist stories,

It'll stop you; I can already tell.

A Gift

We ignore it
And live on.
We stay afraid,
For what reason?

We try to avoid,
Death,
And death is certain.
We prolong life,
Yet we stay just existing.

If death teaches me one thing,
It is to live fully;
Not hoping for a future,
But enjoying the present,
For it is such a gift.

Chances

You can never run out

Of chances

To start

Again.

Dance with what's strange

Life is happening.

It's always present.

To me,

I continually perceive it,

I can hear, I can see.

For some reason,

It seems,

I cannot stay happy,

For the longest of times,

Because, for some reason,

I'm worrying,

Looking for something,

To find.

But it's not the usual.

The thoughts are more diverse.

A questioning of life,

And of life's entire purpose.

I'm on the verge of being happy,

But I'm holding myself back.

I'm latching onto thoughts,

Those ones based in lack.

Questions of how I'm supposed to live,

What I'm supposed to be doing.

Rule books, commandments, ideals,

They've got to be kidding.

There's one thing, I've found,

To do in these times.

To leave validation,

Its own parking fine.

To engage in what's fun,

To join in life's dance.

Boring

I feel like

We need to get

Bashed around a bit,

In life.

Otherwise,

It would get boring.

We're all weirdos

We're all weirdos here.

Don't go braking ankles,

Out of your frequent fears.

We're all spilling toothpaste,

And spitting on ourselves.

With strange intentions,

And creative expressions.

We're all craving here,

Being really weird.

Collecting people, like stamps;

The ones that understand.

Steps can make you taller,

But only for a moment.

The only way to grow,

Is to accept you're paying rent,

In a body, made of lead.

A place for a century.

Is a human, the body?

Or the subtlety?

Where did we all go?

Will we meet again on the road?

We're all weirdos here.

And there's no one who knows.

Death

Do not speak,

Death we do not seek.

I say death is guaranteed,

A magic black spark

Which starts my passion.

A certainty of which,

Leaves me everything.

She's a trickster

She was pointing at me.

She wanted me to fall.

She's a trickster,

She's a fool.

She's tempting,

Persuasive.

She holds her hand out,

To grab me.

She's whispering in my ear,

Taunting me.

Come near.

This is what you want,

I know it.

You can't live without me,

I'll show it.

Wait,

Shush.

I've looked inside,

And I've found,

You disappear.

So, explain to me,

How this works.

You're pulling me sideways,

I want to stay here.

Trying to get me, to play,

With your distractions,

With what you say.

Well, I've found myself.

So, off you go!

Feel free to leave the door open.

And while you're at it,

Leave the others alone.

How they feel

I wonder how they all feel
About death;

The quiet ones' thoughts,
The brave ones' fears.

This Moment

It's right there.

It is BOLD.

It jumps,

It grabs me by the ears.

One second,

Where was I?

One second,

I'm sorry.

It's gone.

Again, and again

We do it again and again,

But say to never repeat,

Because it destroys us;

It makes us feel weak.

It never took long

To forget what you'd done

And start over,

Again, and again.

Dear Mr. President

Your firm grip,

From hands,

Large enough

To hold a country.

Yet your strength is weak,

And we stand on soft skin.

Your worries,

Your desires,

Felt by populations.

With wounds left open,

With blood so thin.

Fame, Fortune, Sin

Toying with my mind,
Thoughts out of control.
All tangled up within,
Fame, fortune, sin.

I want to be taken,
Change me if you like.
There's nothing else for me,
I just want to be liked.

The problem is,
I'm never complete.
Constantly grasping,
At people and things.

So, there's a decision;

A path, I need to take.

Not part of acceptance,

But where I'm awake.

Poison

Sometimes,

You need to be aware

Of the poison,

So, you can avoid

Sipping glasses

Tainted blue.

Everything

Sometimes the toughest thing,

Is accepting you can't do everything.

Strong

I've got a skin

To save me from your hurtful thoughts,

And a warm heart

To keep me strong.

I'm asking for it

Asking for it,

I'm asking for it.

Danger,

Labour,

But, I'm not your saviour.

Unsettled

A strange feeling washed over me.
This feeling of,
Unsettled, confusion.
I felt uneasy.

It's strange how such a feeling,
Can take over.
Leave you weak.
Leave you alone.

I felt dissatisfied,
And strange.
I didn't want to move,
From where I was.
I didn't know
Where to go.

Glass of water

Living with a glass of water
In my mind,
It restricts my room.

I know I must not spill,
To accommodate the water,
To not make the floor slippery,
For others
Not dancing
Through fear.

Until I realised,
I was stood in an ocean.
Dropping glass to sea,
Letting it merge with the rest,
Whilst I jumped up
Took flight and left.

Your Eyes

Does office work,

Fulfil us?

Creatures for motion

And play.

Or does it serve to dampen us,

Slow us,

Into a living Death, of sorts?

I hear your laughter,

But your eyes

See only disaster,

And fear.

Your spark's gone missing,

But it's easy to find,

Just settle into being,

Make peace with your mind.

Dark Times

Even dark times,

Can be seen

In the light.

Where's the funk gone?

Let the water flow;

Tears are liquid gold.

Pure emotion,

No distraction,

I know, I'll grow.

Empowered,

I'm strong.

After much time,

Spent crying,

I feel rejuvenated.

I'm ready to go.

Bring me back my life;

I'm ready to wonder,

Once more.

Being true to myself,

I feel so funky,

Of that, I'm sure.

Find you

I don't want
To sleep,
Not now
I'm running.

I'm scared
I'll never
Find you.

If you leave,
Make sure
You find me.

I live for you,
Without you,
I'm dying.

On the way down

I'll work it out

On the

Way

Down.

Hold my hand

Don't replace love;
Let it be important,
It will carry you through.

Let those things
Which energise you,
Pull you out of bed.

Have faith
In your experience,
Look up.

Fill yourself with power
And hold
My
Hand
Tight.

Finding

Off we go,

Searchlights in hand.

Confident steps.

Anxious sidles.

We stride boldly,

Into unknown territory.

Pathless routes,

Stars are now hiding.

Silence surrounds us,

All busy finding.

Brave

I instantly needed to run.
Instead,
I decided to stay.
This felt like something important.
I couldn't do this,
Not every day.

I owned up to being cowardly;
A simple confession to myself.
Always pointing fingers,
This time I had to listen.

Right against my nature,
I stayed stood, alone.
I had nothing to hide.

Be Strong

Be strong facing

Embarrassment.

Be strong facing

Fear.

I will never stop

Every day, I will get up.

I will do what I must.

I will flow as a river.

On any ground,

At any pace,

Through any valley,

Every day.

And I,

Will never

Stop.

Impossible

Remember when that felt impossible,

You could never have pictured it.

Yet, it happened;

It's now a part of you.

So why are you so unsure to think

Of those great things you want to achieve?

You're a couple of steps away,

But my god, it's closer than you could ever see.

We strive

We run from our thoughts,
Yet indulge in thinking.
We love to feel,
But condone any feeling.

We strive for a future,
When there is only a present.
Working harder and harder
For un-promised pensions.

Why stay miserable
Every moment of now,
As an unpredictable force
Is working your life.

Say no

You can't always tell,

Where this decision,

Will land you.

And I know,

Leaving things be,

It feels easy.

Although,

When the time feels right,

Stand tall

And say no.

The Lies

It was all about learning.

Learning not to listen,

To the lies in my head.

Temptations

Liberation from a game

I've never played.

I see all those signs;

I see you suffering,

It seems so clear.

So easily blinded,

With sugar-coated bullets

You're ready to shoot us.

So tempting with this idea

Of fame

And money.

Loss

Holding on

To what I might lose;

It's a shame really,

When I've got everything to gain.

To have dependency,

To be scared

Of what I might not have.

Yet, not being thankful

For what I've already gotten,

In the past.

I can't help it

At the end of the day,

I can't help being human.

I blamed you

I'd always been quite happy,

In this frame.

If anything went wrong,

Straight back to blame.

Yet, in time,

I came to realise,

It was only myself,

I'd paralysed.

Decisions

I decided to face

The full brunt

Of my decisions.

Uncertain

I was chasing

To make my future,

So that I could

Be settled

And find comfort.

In this world of

Unknown,

Uncertain mysteries,

I must have been blind!

To not see I was

Destroying myself,

My very essence,

I was chasing away.

Running to something

I could never keep

Hold of.

I think this will take to

Holding hands with uncertainty,

And marching forwards.

To accept pain as a challenge,

And a chance to be free.

Say

It's not that I'm hiding it,

It's that you don't know me well enough to figure it out.

And maybe I don't even know.

So, telling you isn't possible.

There's no way to say it.

Lying to you

So, I'm sorry for lying
Or keeping the truth.
It was only these fears,
Keeping lying so near.

And since I've nothing to hide,
Here's the three things,
I've wanted to tell you.
Three things I needed to do.

Falling

It's something
I could never say;
The thoughts,
Those in my head.

They shout
And scream.
They're heavy,
Like lead.

I'm ready
To be thrown,
As long as you're there.

If you're not here

To catch me,

I'll be falling

Forever.

Jealous

Do you live in a jealous land?

Is my grass greener,

Than the one in your hand?

Do you speak in a jealous tone?

Is the music you play,

More deep, more alone?

I can see that you're jealous,

I can see I am too.

Maybe, one day, we'll see

This isn't the way

To set ourselves free.

Oncoming Traffic

There's a fine line,

Between

Sprinting down the road,

And falling

Into oncoming traffic.

Wafer Thin

It's that feeling again:
The faintness of existence,
The un-promised future,
The thinnest line,
Being here, and not.

It swarms me,
It cuddles me
Sometimes too hard,
And I suffocate.

I feel wafer thin,
So very mortal.
This feeling is becoming familiar,
Yet never quite feels comfortable.

Naked

I realised,

If I took off my jumper,

I'd be naked inside.

There's a kind of mess,

I can leave,

When no one's around.

Free of beliefs,

I can live as I am.

Being strange,

Unpredictable.

No place, I can't stand.

The incident

I must be wary,

As it seems

My brain keeps incidentally

Putting me in competition

With everyone else.

Conclusions

Humans built,

To jump into conclusions.

Minds working overtime,

A recipe for confusion.

I know nothing

We worry ourselves,
Of what isn't yet here.
Thinking of a future
Totally unclear.

Seen as it shall, always be
Uncertain,
I think I shall dive
Headfirst;

To see its offerings,
To live its mysteries,
I am excited for life,
For I know nothing.

So, there is everything

To discover.

"Beeboo"

The metamorphic soft lump of podgy curiosity. Beeboo is a very expressive little character, he doesn't know very much but he feels very deeply and loves to wreak havoc, even if by accident.

Beeboo found his way to me one cold evening. At the time I was very into textiles and sewing, I loved making clothes and feeling all the different fabrics. But, on that evening, it seemed nothing wanted to be created. I couldn't find any inspiration whatsoever and I sat at my sewing machine gloomy and in a total grump. It's strange how in these moments you can feel totally unworthy, totally sad. Looking back, these were some of my most thoughtful times, some of the most melancholic but also beautiful. And this is when Beeboo came along. In a dazed numbness, I found my most favourite fabric out of the mound of cloths and cottons in front of me: a super soft white blanket. The type of blanket you snuggle under in those lost moments. As I picked it up, it glided across my fingers, the softness so comforting. Without rulers or measurements, I began to cut the fabric in this way and that, imperfections totally welcomed! I sewed one piece to another, snipped some off one side, popped a needle and thread in the other. When I had a shape, I decided that I wanted this creature to have some weight, so I filled him with linseed and threw some lemon and lavender oil into his belly before patching him up. I held him in my hands, outstretched in front of me, and there was this curious looking, kind, lumpy thing. I can't remember how he got his name; it was just him. He was a Beeboo, and that night he taught me something very important. He taught me the importance of feeling.

AND THERE'S MORE!

For more poetry, creations and imperfect things, follow me on Instagram at:

@tigerinblue

For burning questions, getting in touch and yelling at me to get a wider variety of social media accounts:

leannaamos29@hotmail.com

I also have a rogue photography page if you get excited and want to see more of what I'm up to.

@shotbyleanna

If Beeboo has captured your heart like he did mine, or even if you thought he was just a soppy podgy lump, here's where you'll find all things him:

@beeboothelump

Additionally, head to this online location to mooch on all things writing, reading and publishing. Feel free to join the wonderful community of writers and readers involved in the Sleepy Lion blog, and even try your hand at dreaming and write a book and get it published here too!

www.sleepylionpublishing.com

SLEEPY LION

PUBLISHING

If you are interested in publishing, writing and you love to read, then head over to
www.sleepylionpublishing.com

Otherwise, all questions can be sent to
enquiries@sleepylionpublishing.com

If you would like to submit any work, whether a short story, article, blog post or even art work, then send us an email at submissions@sleepylionpublishing.com

We offer different payed contracts on smaller pieces, so whether you would rather an upfront payment, or to make money over time, we also personalise our collaborations. So, get in contact now and start earning money from your work!

On our website you will find:

-Our personal editing, illustrating and publishing services

- Blog posts

-Articles on writing and reading

-Essays

-Short Stories

-Book Covers

-Poetry

-Exciting Merchandise

-Contests (Coming soon!)

-Magazines (Coming soon!)

-News on any books we are publishing

(Poetry on Beauty: coming soon!)

(Poetry on Art: coming soon!)

To a future of creativity, wonder and all things playful!

Printed in Great Britain
by Amazon